For Ben, Eve, Richard and Sammy

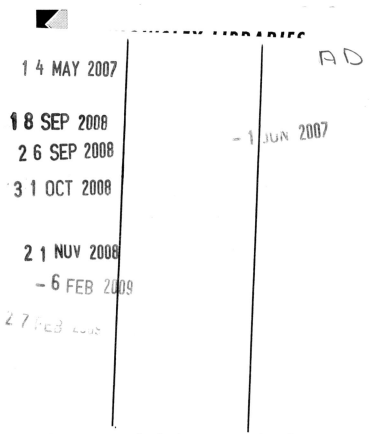

Eric Taplin was Head of Department of Social Studies at Liverpool Polytechnic (now Liverpool John Moores University) from 1972 to 1984. He is now a Fellow of the University of Liverpool in the Department of Economic and Social History. His particular research interest is in British labour history, especially the development of industrial relations in Liverpool. He was a founder member of the North West Group for the Study of Labour History and is its chairperson. He is the author of *Liverpool Dockers and Seamen, 1870-1890* (1974) and *The Dockers' Union. A Study of the National Union of Dock Labourers, 1889-1922* (1985).

The Carbonora postcard collection and copies of the Liverpool Daily Post and Mercury are held in the Liverpool Record Office (Liverpool City Council, Libraries and Arts Department).
Four of the photographs used are held in the Photography Department of the National Museums and Galleries on Merseyside.
Copies of the Liverpool Weekly Post and The Sphere magazine were consulted in the British Museum Newspaper Library, Colindale.
I am grateful for permission to reproduce the photographs from these sources.

Cover photograph	Armoured police van
	(Carbonora)
	Hand colouring
	by Peter Turner

First published	The Bluecoat Press
1994	Bluecoat Chambers
	School Lane
	Liverpool L1 3BX

Text ©	Eric Taplin
Designed by	March design
Printed by	Printeksa
	ISBN 1 872568 14 9

NEAR TO REVOLUTION

THE LIVERPOOL GENERAL TRANSPORT STRIKE OF 1911

Eric Taplin

THE BLUECOAT PRESS

Preface

This book of photographs is a contribution to the growing interest in the local history of Merseyside. There have been many publications on the economic history of the region with an emphasis on the great firms, especially in shipping, notable public figures and the role they played in the furious expansion of the region before the First World War. Only recently, however, has there developed an equal interest in the contribution made by working people, their lifestyles, their problems and their efforts to secure a decent standard of living. The success of the publications of the *Docklands History Project* of the University of Liverpool and those of the *History and Society of Merseyside* series, a joint venture between the University of Liverpool, the Liverpool John Moores University and Countyvise under the imprint of the Liver Press, show that the people of Merseyside are eager to learn about the lives and work of their predecessors.

Although this book will be of particular interest to Merseysiders I am hopeful that it will also appeal to those who do not know the region but who have an interest in social and labour history. The events examined and the pictorial record presented depict a labour dispute that was of more than parochial interest in that it formed part of a national crisis in labour relations before the First World War.

The Liverpool General Strike of 1911 was, arguably, the most momentous event in Liverpool's labour history. Between June and August of that year the city virtually came to a standstill during a prolonged industrial dispute. I have provided an introduction outlining the major features of the labour unrest that swept across the country in the years immediately before the First World War. This is followed by a brief examination and analysis of the Liverpool strike that formed part of the national militancy.

The strength of the book is, however, the collection of photographs taken during the strike. Most of them were the work of photographers of the local firm of Carbonora. I have provided some information on the photographic collection with a commentary accompanying each plate. I hope this material will make the photographic collection more valuable and interesting to readers than would otherwise be the case. I have also included copies of documents that illustrate the importance of the conflict both locally and nationally.

Many people have been of assistance to me in preparing this book though I hold none responsible for its shortcomings. My greatest debt is to the Liverpool City Council Libraries and Arts Department and in particular to Janet Smith, City Archivist. Her help and support made this book possible. Ian Qualtrough and Susan Yee of the Photographic Unit of the University of Liverpool were responsible for the reprocessing of the photographs and their expertise was invaluable. Pat Ayers, formerly research worker in the *Docklands History Project*, kindly drew my attention to the two certificates (Documents 5 and 6). Paul Laxton of the Department of Geography at the university advised me on the maps and I thank Sandra Mather and Paul Smith for preparing them. Harold Hikins was generous in allowing me to use documents concerning the strike that are in his possession and Paul Cosgrove of the Kirkby Unemployed Centre provided me with valuable information. John Mills, managing director of John Mills Photography Ltd., whose grandfather founded Carbonora, generously provided me with material on the firm's history. My colleagues in the Department of Economic and Social History at the university have been a constant source of encouragement. In particular I thank Pat Hudson who first suggested that the collection deserved a wider audience than those attending an Open Day at the university where they were first exhibited. She was also good enough to read a draft of the introduction and provided me with valuable comments. I am grateful to Marij Van Helmond, Curator of Social and Labour History at the Museum of Liverpool Life, for her generous and enthusiastic support and to Michael Stammers, Keeper of the Merseyside Maritime Museum. I acknowledge with thanks the generous financial support given by the trustees of the Lipman Trust. Finally, it is appropriate to pay tribute to Gwilym Mills, the owner of the firm of Carbonora, who in 1911 captured so vividly the spirit of a city in crisis through the photographs contained in this book.

Over the last fifteen years trade unions in Britain have been driven on to the defensive by successive Conservative governments. Anti-union legislation has led to a loss of influence, membership and status. This is not the first time in British history that organised labour has faced severe challenges and I am hopeful that this book will be a timely reminder of the rich heritage of struggle by working people to secure protection against the excesses of 'market forces' through the strength and influence of the trade union movement.

Eric Taplin
February 1994

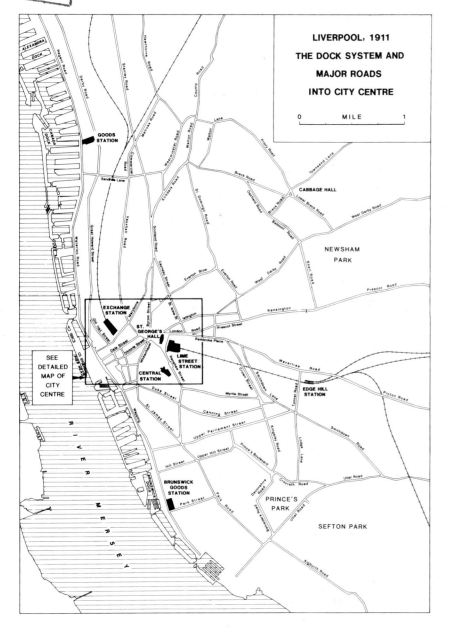

LIVERPOOL, 1911

THE DOCK SYSTEM AND

MAJOR ROADS

INTO CITY CENTRE

0   MILE   1

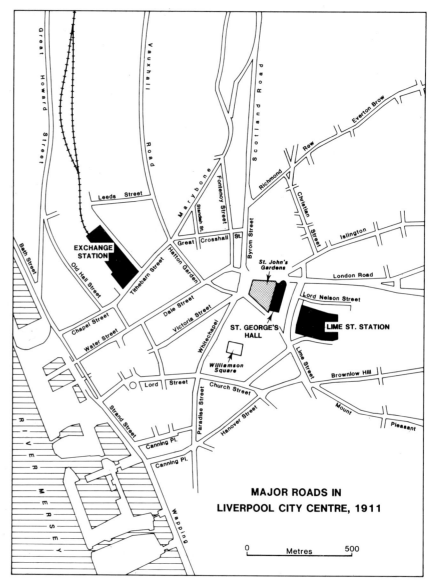

MAJOR ROADS IN
LIVERPOOL CITY CENTRE, 1911

0   Metres   500

Introduction

The Labour Unrest, 1911 - 1914 and the Liverpool General Transport Strike of 1911

The efforts of ordinary people to improve their standard of life and to secure greater dignity and recognition of their role in society have been evident in British history since at least the Peasants' Revolt of 1381. The impact of the Industrial Revolution in the eighteenth and nineteenth centuries sharpened those efforts. Industrialisation and the growth of foreign trade in the nineteenth century made Britain the wealthiest nation in the world. Economic and political power was retained, however, in the hands of the landed aristocracy and the owners and manipulators of capital in manufacturing, commerce and trade. Working people may have enjoyed a higher standard of living than their predecessors but there remained large pools of degradation and those without work for any length of time suffered grievously.

The spread of the factory system, urbanisation and a rapidly rising population contributed to a growing conflict between the owners of capital and working people. Few legislative controls restrained employers and in the factory and workshop there were persistent controversies over such issues as work discipline, hours and conditions of work, rates of pay and manning levels. The new industrial towns and cities were overwhelmed by migrants from rural areas and from overseas, especially Ireland, intensifying the problems of housing and public health which had always been associated with urban areas. The rising population provided a vast supply of labour, most of whom lacked the education and skill to undertake the more specialist, higher paid and secure jobs that were available. In the labour market, therefore, there were sharp distinctions between the skilled and the unskilled. Craftsmen enjoyed a higher and more regular income with relative security of employment. But only a small proportion of the working population was in that privileged position. For most workers wages were low and irregular and bouts of under-employment and unemployment were part of the fabric of life.

Aug 1911

Workers of Liverpool

Have not the events of the last few days proved to you that there are only two parties—

THE WORKERS AND THEIR ENEMIES

Liberal and Tory have alike shown themselves in their true colours. Will you remember this when next election time comes round, or will you vote blindly, as in the past, for the **Master Class?**

Socialism is a plan which will give the worker the just reward of his labour.

The results of the present system you have before you.

SOCIALISM IS THE ONLY REMEDY

All workers, moreover, faced pressures from employers who sought to reduce costs and raise productivity. Most manufacturers were competing among themselves for markets and increasingly foreign competition in both the domestic and overseas markets drove them to seek greater efficiency of operation. In many occupations work discipline became more harsh and rates of pay were constantly under pressure. Workers secured some tardy protection by legislation such as the factory acts but successive governments distanced themselves from industrial affairs. It was not until 1886 that the Labour Department of the Board of Trade was established to collect and disseminate statistical data on industrial relations. Another decade passed before the Conciliation Act of 1896 provided opportunities for the Board of Trade to appoint conciliators to help resolve industrial disputes and not until the first decade of the twentieth century that the government involved itself directly in major industrial conflicts.

Working people had, therefore, to rely upon their own efforts to resist the excesses of industrial capitalism and to secure higher standards of living. Demonstrations and riots had frequently taken place against those who were largely indifferent or hostile to the aspirations of the poor but in a developing industrialised society the strike became the most common form of protest and the lock-out the employers' usual response. Increasingly, and especially from the 1850s, the development of national and regional trade unions and the growth of formal and informal employers' associations institutionalised the conflicts of labour and capital though the penetration of union organisation was patchy. As might be expected skilled workers were more successful than the unskilled in forming permanent organisations, wresting concessions from employers, enjoying a measure of recognition and the establishment in some cases of collective bargaining procedures. For most of the unskilled these were goals that remained to be achieved by 1900 in spite of efforts throughout the century, some of which had been briefly successful.[1]

The vast majority of strikes and lock-outs that have taken place have faded from public interest or remembrance though they generated excitement at the time. Some, however, have become benchmarks in the history of the labour movement either because they initiated significant change in industrial relations or because they led to new trade union structures or because they were associated with new ideologies or strategies.

One such benchmark was the labour unrest in the years immediately before the First World War. Conflicts took place in a number of industries on a scale and intensity rarely witnessed before. Many were prolonged and bitterly contested involving clashes between the strikers and the police. In some cases the military was brought in to assist in the protection of property. It was among the less skilled that militancy was most pronounced especially among seafarers, railwaymen, coalminers and waterfront workers. In these occupations, except the coalminers, trade unionism was less well developed, membership was patchy and the employment of blacklegs more easily secured by employers, encouraging clashes between strikers and 'free labour'. This has led some scholars to suggest that the labour unrest was the fulfilment of the upsurge of 'New Unionism' of the late 1880s which led to the establishment of trade unionism among the unskilled

on a scale not witnessed before but which had been cut short by adverse economic conditions and a successful employers' counter-attack in the 1890s.[2]

Other historians, however, have emphasised the broad range of industries, crafts and skills affected by pointing to disputes in coalmining, cotton textiles and the building industry. Indeed Joe White has claimed that there were 'two concurrent labour unrests during the years 1910-14': disputes involving the 'hitherto unorganised and unrecognised' and those 'waged by workers who were already members of established and recognised unions...'[3]

The labour unrest led to a considerable increase in trade union membership. In 1909 about two and a half million people belonged to trade unions; in 1914 there were over four millions. Some unions, like the Dock, Wharf, Riverside and General Labourers' Union which had been virtually eliminated from the London docks in the 1890s, were now revived. Others that had been recently established, such as the Workers' Union, recruited in large numbers. Many employers were forced to make significant concessions, sometimes involving the recognition of unions; and the government's chief conciliator, George Askwith, was at full stretch in seeking to resolve disputes that were fought with such intransigence. In 1913 he could not see the unrest coming to an end:

'That the present unrest will cease I do not believe for one moment; it will increase, and probably increase with greater force. Within a comparatively short time there may be movements in this country coming to a head of which recent events have been a small foreshadowing.'[4]

Askwith's forebodings were not realised. The outbreak of war in August 1914 brought the unrest to an end. Ernest Bevin, like Askwith, believed that but for the war the escalation of conflict would have continued leading to 'one of the greatest industrial revolts the world would ever have seen'.[5]

The causes of the industrial unrest have been much debated by contemporaries and historians. To some Britain was experiencing an underlying crisis in spite of the superficial glitter of the Edwardian era. George Dangerfield developed an interpretation first put forward by Elie Halevy[6] 'that by the end of 1913 Liberal England was reduced to ashes.' The constitutional crisis of 1910, the suffragette movement, the labour unrest, the question of Irish Home Rule and the drift towards the international crisis that led to the First World War signalled the end of an era.[7]

Most historians have reacted sceptically to a 'society in crisis' interpretation. Economistic explanations stress that wage rates were not keeping pace with prices. As real wages fell so a sense of grievance developed among workers which sought release through strike action. Important in this may have been the attempts made to cut wages by some employers in the depression that preceded the inflation of 1911-13: the industrial disputes of 1908 confirm the refusal of many workers to accept lower wages. George Askwith claimed that 'the ... principal causes of the disputes ... were either economic demands for better wages and conditions, or arose from the pressing forward of organisation too fast in the idea that organisation, however obtained, was necessary to obtain economic improvements'.[8]

Henry Pelling has drawn attention to the impact of the trade cycle. Unemployment fell sharply during the years of good trade from 1911 so that 'men could more readily defy their employers when the supply of potential blacklegs was at its lowest'.[9] Such defiance, it has been argued, may have been encouraged by social factors. A growing sense of indignation emerged among working people as conspicuous consumption by the rich became more evident through the spread of the tabloid press. Photographs and gossip columns recorded vividly the luxurious life-style of the better off though it would be fanciful to accept George Askwith's belief in the inflammatory effects upon the working classes of the growing use of the motor car by the rich.[10]

Hugh Clegg has recently analysed fourteen of the most notable disputes between 1910 and 1914. He concluded that while the fall in real wages since 1900 must have had a considerable influence on the attitude of wage earners, two other factors were of major importance. Firstly, there was a boom in union organisation similar to those of 1871-73 and 1889-90 and, secondly, there was a determination of some employers to resist wage demands. In the latter case Clegg considers that coalowners and railway companies in particular were in an 'adverse cost position ... which, in terms of their current wage agreements, impelled them to reject what might otherwise have been considered not unreasonable demands'.[11]

The boom in organisation is undeniable but it is more properly seen as an effect rather than a cause of the industrial unrest. Why did workers join trade unions in such large numbers? Considerable importance can be placed on the work process. In some industries work discipline was being forced upon employees with increasing rigour. The upturn in trade gave employers an opportunity to increase profits. By working their employees harder they were able to confine the employment of extra 'hands' to a minimum. Certainly on the docks the tyranny of foremen rose markedly even though more jobs were available. Resentment against the disturbance of traditional work patterns was bound to grow and with real wages falling - aggravated by social discontents - many workers were ripe for militant protest which they perceived as most likely to be successful through trade union organisation.

Political explanations have normally been associated with

the development of syndicalism. Workers control by direct action was encouraged by Tom Mann, the most magnetic labour activist of the time. G.D.H. Cole and Raymond Postgate claimed that the attraction of syndicalism derived from the lack of will within parliament to grant a greater share of wealth to the workers. The newly-formed Labour Party as part of the parliamentary system failed to live up to the expectations of those who sought fundamental social and economic reforms and, hence, 'the resort to direct action by one body of trade unionists after another'.[12] There is little evidence, however, to support this conclusion. Syndicalism won support among a minority of workers and few, if any, unions explicitly adopted a syndicalist policy. Syndicalist groups within unions sought to influence policy but without much success.[13] In any case the issue of industrial solidarity, one of the hallmarks of syndicalism, was espoused by many labour leaders as a sensible strategy though they were opposed or indifferent to syndicalist theory.

The causes of the industrial unrest remain unresolved emphasising 'the elusive quality of the pre-war turbulence'.[14] Any monocausal interpretation must be treated with scepticism. What can be said is that workers had plenty of grievances. Those in weakly organised industries poured into unions demanding recognition and union pay and conditions. Those in well-organised industries such as coal and cotton had grievances about the constraints imposed by collective bargaining agreements reached between the union bureaucracy and the employers. As firms grew in size and as profit-making opportunities increased, management became more remote and harsher work discipline was imposed. Social grievances sharpened the mood of discontent.

Finally, a word of caution is necessary. Although it is undeniable that the industrial unrest generated a good deal of excitement and led to a marked expansion in trade union membership, Richard Hyman has pointed out that the large majority of workers in the country did not take part in the pre-war industrial unrest: 'by 1914 three quarters of them remained outside the ranks of trade unionists'.[15] Also Hugh Clegg has suggested that what made the period memorable was not the widespread nature of strike activity but the 'small number of large strikes'.[16] It might be added, however, that these large conflicts were in key industries like coalmining, railways, shipping and dock work which appeared to threaten the basic fabric of the economy.

The photograph below shows police, soldiers and possibly 'blacklegs' on board a ship in the Mersey. The actual significance of such a grouping is not clear. (NMGM)

The Liverpool General Transport Strike Of 1911

This is the national context within which the Liverpool General Transport Strike of 1911 took place, one of the most serious and prolonged disputes of the pre-war labour unrest. It was probably the most important industrial dispute that the city had experienced. Industrial relations were fundamentally altered as a result of the strike and the short-term reverberations persisted up until the outbreak of the First World War. The dispute was a series of overlapping conflicts involving seamen, ships' stewards and catering staff, dock labourers, carters, tugboatmen, coalheavers, ancillary waterfront workers (such as cold storage men and boiler scalers), railwaymen, tramwaymen, electric power station workers and scavengers (dustmen and street cleaners). The seamen initiated the conflict by turning out on June 14. In mid-August, a general strike was successfully organised and some 66,000 workers were involved bringing the city to a virtual standstill. It was not until August 25 that the last group of workers, the dock labourers, returned to work and not until December 1911, that the reinstatement of corporation tramwaymen was completed.

Contemporaries testified to the impact of the strike. Margaret Postgate had just left school at eighteen years of age. In her autobiography she recalled 'what was almost a small civil war ... I remember a broiling August ... the stench of the unscavenged streets - the Corporation employees came out in sympathy - and of the truckloads of vegetables rotting at Edge Hill station. I remember bits of broken bottle, relics of battles down by the Docks, the rain-patter of feet walking the pavements when the trams ceased to run and clank, the grey *Antrim* lying on guard in the Mersey, the soldiers marching through the streets, special editions of the evening papers coming out every half-hour, and American tourists, decanted from the *Baltic*, sitting at Pier Head on their Saratoga trunks with no porters to carry them away.'[17]

Philip Gibbs was a journalist, 'an observer and recorder of contemporary life with critical but not hostile eyes'. In his autobiography he called the Liverpool strike 'as near to a revolution as anything I had seen in England. It started with a strike of the transport workers, and spread to other unions who declared sympathetic strikes. For many weeks - nearly three months - nothing moved in Liverpool. The railway porters came out. The tramwaymen were idle. Even the road sweepers declined to work. Some troops were sent into the city to maintain order but increased disorder because they were stoned by the strikers and were not allowed to fire in self-defence. They had to retreat under showers of kidney stones with which the mob armed themselves. The situation was alarming and not without brutality among the strikers, whose passions were aroused.'[18]

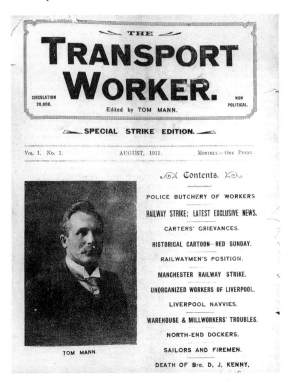

The passions of the workers were aroused because they had long-standing grievances of low pay, harsh work discipline, insecurity of employment and belligerent employers with strong anti-union sentiments. The drafting into the city of troops and of extra police from elsewhere intensified feelings of resentment. The conflict was, nevertheless, a success for the workers. All except the tramwaymen secured concessions, some of a significant nature. A number of unions, notably those for the seafarers and the dockers, were recognised by the shipping companies and union conditions and rates of pay successfully negotiated. It would, however, be misleading to suggest that the employers were simply crushed. They were forced to adopt new strategies that embraced union recognition but they demanded that union leaders exert a greater discipline over their members. Among dock labourers, for example, precipitate strike action was now denied to work groups. Grievances had to be channelled through an agreed procedure during which men were to stay at work. The union was to 'police' the agreement and if it was unable to control its members the employers could threaten withdrawal.

The chronology of the strike is complex but may be briefly summarised as follows:

June 14 to August 4. The seamen came out on strike followed by ships' catering staff and stewards. The north end dock labourers[19] and the carters also struck work in sympathy with the seafarers in what was an exclusively waterfront demonstration of solidarity. A strike committee was formed, chaired by Tom Mann, consisting of representatives of the unions involved and of the Liverpool Trades Council. The major steamship companies were the first to be approached and to grant concessions to the seafarers, followed by the smaller firms. But to the surprise of the employers the north end non-union dockers now demanded recognition of the dockers' union and union rates of pay and conditions. They flocked to enrol in the National Union of Dock Labourers (NUDL). The coalheavers, who had their own unions, followed suit. Reluctant though the shipping firms were to grant recognition to the NUDL the big firms submitted when the seafarers struck work again in sympathy with the dockers. Employees were permitted to wear the union badge at the stands and at work and a conference was arranged to hammer out a permanent settlement with the union. The final meeting took place on August 4 and led to the publication of the *White Book Agreement,* a document containing details of the settlement. It was a major victory for the union. The dockers' union - and the two seafarers' unions - were fully recognised and wages were enhanced. Union dockers received preference of employment at the hiring stands although it was not formally written into the *White Book Agreement.* Any man who sought regular employment was obliged to join the union and display his union badge or 'button'. A joint committee was established consisting of employer and union representatives in equal number to resolve any disputes by negotiation. In return the NUDL agreed to guarantee continuity of work while any dispute was being resolved through the joint committee. The seafarers' victory was less complete but the stranglehold exercised by the Shipping Federation was broken and some of its more objectionable practices abandoned.

August 7-25. Discontent among railwaymen had been mounting nationally and the success of the waterfront workers encouraged Liverpool railwaymen to seek concessions. Some 4,000 railwaymen struck work on 7 August demanding reduced hours and increased wages. Railwaymen were co-opted on to the strike committee and it was agreed that all transport workers would support them through sympathetic action. At this the shipping employers lost all patience with the dock labourers. Within a few days of signing an agreement guaranteeing continuity of work a major stoppage was threatened. An ultimatum was issued to the NUDL demanding that the *White Book Agreement* be honoured so that union members remained at work. If not all cargo operations in the port would cease on August 14 - the men would be locked out.

Matters were brought to a head, however, on Sunday, August 13. A monster demonstration took place at St. George's Plateau, in the centre of Liverpool, organised by the strike committee in support of the railwaymen. Some 80,000 people attended. As the speeches began there was a small disturbance nearby in Lord Nelson Street, the origins of which have never been firmly established. The authorities panicked and police who had been hidden in St. George's Hall were let loose and repeatedly baton-charged the crowds until the plateau was cleared. There were no deaths but hundreds were injured. A contingent of the Warwickshire Regiment was posted in Lime Street once the police had cleared the area and the Riot Act was read by the city stipendiary magistrate. This was followed by a night of looting and battles with the police. The Riot Act was read a second time as pitched battles took place between the police and groups

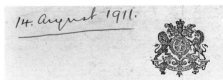

14. August 1911.

With a loud voice.

COMMAND SILENCE

while Proclamation is making.

Our Sovereign Lady the Queen

chargeth and commandeth all persons, being assembled, immediately to disperse themselves, and peaceably to depart to their habitations, or to their lawful business, upon the pains contained in the Act made in the 1st year of King George for preventing Tumults and Riotous Assemblies.

GOD SAVE THE QUEEN.

of people who were intent on looting shops and pubs. Near Great Homer Street sectarian conflicts flared up and the police again baton-charged the crowds. Up until then violence had been minimal considering the large numbers involved in the strikes but from then on attitudes hardened, the relationship between the police and the public deteriorated and ' "Bloody Sunday" came to symbolise the intolerance of an apprehensive civil authority towards peaceful mass demonstration.'[20]

In the course of the next week Liverpool virtually came to a standstill. The shipowners locked out their cargo handlers, the

Soldiers at the Threshold.

LIVERPOOL STRIKE-RIDDEN

LORD MAYOR MAY CALL OUT MILITARY.

15,000 MEN IN REVOLT.

POLICE REINFORCEMENTS STONED.

REPEATED BATON CHARGES.

RIOTERS ARRESTED.

SUGGESTED BOARD OF TRADE MEDIATION.

strike committee called for a general turn out and up to 66,000 people responded. The strike committee issued permits for the carriage of essential goods; all others could only be moved under heavy police and military escort. On August 17 a national strike of railwaymen began which lasted for three days before the railway companies were persuaded to meet union representatives to discuss grievances. Also on August 17 the Liverpool tramwaymen struck work followed by Corporation electric power station workers and the scavengers.

The resolution of the railwaymen's dispute at national level heralded the end of the local transport strike. The dockers finally returned to work on August 25 following negotiations between the NUDL and the shipping employers. But the tramwaymen who had struck work were dismissed and the Corporation Tramways Committee only agreed to reinstatement when the strike committee threatened to bring out all transport workers again. Reinstatement was, however, tardily undertaken and was not finally completed until December 1911.

There are four factors of the dispute worthy of comment: the solidarity of the strikers, the crucial role of unorganised workers, the impact of the strike on industrial relations at the waterfront, and the response of the civil authorities to the conflict.

Firstly, the solidarity shown by work groups was unprecedented. The seamen (deck hands and engine room workers) refused to return to work until the ships' catering staffs and stewards had secured comparable concessions; the dockers initially turned out in support of the seafarers, the latter in turn supporting the dockers in their claim for union recognition; the carters supported both seafarers and dockers; and all these groups - and others - turned out in sympathetic support for the railwaymen and tramwaymen. There was, of course, an element of spontaneity in that the growing excitement and the initial success of the seamen encouraged others to take militant action. More important, however, was the fact that all the work groups involved were ripe for revolt. They had grievances that had been festering for years. What was required was a spark to ignite the explosion. It was provided by the impetuous decision of Joseph Havelock Wilson, the seamen's leader, to call a national strike. He took an enormous gamble in that his union, the National Sailors' and Firemen's Union (NSFU) was small and weak. He had, indeed, sought for some months to secure negotiations with the employers but the powerful Shipping Federation dismissed all peaceful overtures. In Liverpool and elsewhere the gamble paid off because non-union seamen responded as enthusiastically to Wilson's strike call as his union members. The unexpected support received from the ships' stewards and catering staffs was a great boost to their morale. The stewards had long considered themselves superior to the deck hands and the men who toiled in the stokeholds. But the stewards had serious grievances too. In 1909 Joe Cotter had successfully formed the National Union of Ships' Stewards, Cooks, Butchers and Bakers so the men now 'had an organisation that could articulate their grievances on a port-wide basis'.[21] When Cotter's members supported the seamen it was the first time that seafarers had acted in unison.

Other work groups witnessing this unexpected turn of events were encouraged to seize the opportunity to express their own grievances. They were, of course, influenced by the superb oratory and reputation of Tom Mann and the rapid establishment of a strike committee representing all work groups involved to organise the protest and maintain the momentum of industrial solidarity. Although this had syndicalist overtones it was supported by all members of the committee, most of whom were not syndicalists, because it was an essential strategy for victory.

Secondly, why did non-union labour show such aggression and an enthusiasm for union organisation? It should be remembered that this was the third effort to achieve mass union organisation among the unskilled workers of Merseyside. In 1879/80 efforts made by seamen and dock workers had failed.[22] Greater success was secured in the late 1880s during the upsurge of New Unionism when the NUDL and the National Amalgamated Sailors' and Firemen's Union (NASFU) were formed. But by the mid-1890s the NASFU had collapsed under the onslaught of the Shipping Federation and its successor, the NSFU, was weak and ineffective. Similarly, unemployment and employer hostility had confined the influence of the NUDL to the smaller master stevedore and master porter firms found particularly at the south end of the Liverpool docks.[23] But the initial militancy of the dock labourers in 1911 came from the non-union men who worked for the giant steamship companies at the north end of the docks rather than from the unionised men. For over twenty years firms like Cunard and the White Star Line had banned union labour, any man discovered belonging to the NUDL being instantly dismissed. The work discipline imposed by foremen was fearsome. Bullying and corruption were widespread and men were driven unmercifully. The casual system of employment buttressed by the abundant supply of labour encouraged malpractices. In an effort to gain some influence at the north end the NUDL established a branch there in 1908. It operated in semi-clandestine fashion and had no more than 200 members but its influence was considerable. Preparatory work had, therefore, preceded the events of 1911. Once the seafarers struck work the dockers seized the opportunity to pay off old scores that had been festering for years. They flocked into the union as an act of defiance against their oppressors perceiving the union as the means by which their status, pay and conditions could be improved and the excesses of foremen tyranny constrained.

Seafarers were subject to harsh discipline on board ship, were employed casually, received low wages (which were often reduced by petty fines) and worked excessive hours. For over twenty years the powerful employers' Shipping Federation had dominated their working lives ensuring that no man secured employment without a Federation 'ticket'. Known agitators and union members were weeded out and the Federation possessed strike breaking facilities through the ready supply of blacklegs. Catering staff were additionally threatened by the recruitment of cheap foreign labour.

Railwaymen and tramwaymen had long suffered from a quasi-military work discipline. Both jobs had their attraction, however, in that men were employed permanently rather than casually, there were promotion prospects and a uniform was provided; but the hours of work were horrendous and they were poorly paid. Employers treated the unions with contemptuous hostility.

Thus all the major work groups that took part in the conflict had long-standing grievances. Those who had been deterred by fear of dismissal from expressing complaint were caught up in the excitement of the occasion and, encouraged by the determination and success of other work groups, demanded freedom to join a trade union and pressed for union recognition. The solidity of revolt denied employers their traditional weapon of using local blackleg labour to crush strikes, forcing them to reassess their labour relations.

Thirdly, the impact of the strike upon industrial relations at the waterfront was profound. Before the strike some 8,000 dockers were members of the Merseyside branches of the NUDL. By the end of 1911 there were 31,000 members. This was partly the result of north end dockers and other unorganised work groups such as the cold storage men enrolling and partly the decision of some smaller sectional unions, such as coalheavers, joining the organisation *en bloc*. Other unions, like the NSFU, enjoyed enhanced membership and a more secure influence. Liverpool became the best organised port in the country. Employers were forced to come to terms with the new situation. Alfred Booth, the vigorous young chairman of Cunard, forced employers to act in unison during the strike which led ultimately to the foundation of the powerful Employers' Association of the Port of Liverpool in 1913. A new pattern of industrial relations was established whereby union recognition was granted but continuity of work while disputes were resolved by negotiation was successfully demanded by employers. It became almost impossible to get a job on the waterfront without a union ticket but men could no longer resort to lightning walk-outs, a factor that intensified bickering between the union leadership and the rank and file.

In the long term the 1911 strike proved to be a turning point in industrial relations in Liverpool. For much of the nineteenth century trade unionism in the city had been weak, fragmented, unstable and largely ineffective[24] but, following the recognition of the waterfront unions, belonging to a union became part of the fabric of life for blue collar workers in the city and the depth of union penetration was very impressive. Indeed, the enthusiasm of the rank and file for their unions, their determination and militancy was often greater than those who led them. The individualism endemic to casualism when directed into collective action proved to be a formidable force that branch officials and union executives often found difficult to contain. The strength of union membership among blue collar workers in Liverpool today and their reputation for militancy can be traced back to the dramatic events of 1911.

Fourthly, the response of the civil authorities to the dispute though predictable was inept and counter-productive. In spite of the large number of men on strike, the incidence of violence was small until the catastrophe of Bloody Sunday. A few small fires had broken out on a couple of ships and a steward had been arrested. Minor scuffles had taken place as blacked goods were moved. But relationships between the strikers and the local police remained reasonable. Nevertheless the civil authorities grew alarmed as the strike escalated. Extra police were drafted in from Leeds and Birmingham and over 2,300

troops from six regiments were ultimately camped in the city.

The impact of extra forces heightened rather than reduced tension. It was the police from Leeds and Birmingham who were let loose on the crowds on St. George's Plateau on August 13. From then on they and the military became a convenient target for disaffected individuals and groups and encouraged the revival of sectarian violence which up until then had lain dormant during the industrial struggle. It is not without significance that the two deaths that occurred during the dispute took place when troops were escorting five prison vans along an unaccustomed route to Walton Gaol through the dock area. A dock labourer and a carter were shot dead as the convoy was attacked by 'a mob'. On August 19 a warship, *HMS Antrim*, suddenly appeared anchored in the Mersey. What purpose a gunboat was to serve is difficult to fathom. Was Liverpool to be bombarded or was this a return to Palmerstonian diplomacy of sending in a warship to quell the natives? Whatever the reason within a few days it sailed away as mysteriously as it had arrived.

Once the strike was over and life returned to normal there was work for all to clear shipping and move the goods piled up on quayside and in warehouses. Men were eager to secure income after weeks of deprivation. The agreements hammered out during the conflict were maintained. Indeed, the union executives were anxious to consolidate the *concordat* reached with the employers. But the rank and file among the dockers rapidly appreciated that their freedom to take unilateral action to redress grievances was no longer open to them and congress and executive meetings of the NUDL were even more stormy than they had been in the past. James Sexton, the general secretary, had long been a target for criticism and his

RED RIOT.

Appalling Scenes in Liverpool.

FIERCE BATTLE in Lime Street.

Crowds Charged by the Police

HUNDREDS INJURED.

RIOT ACT READ.

TROOPS CALLED OUT.

MR. TOM MANN'S THREAT.

GENERAL STRIKE TO-MORROW.

AT DEATH GRIPS.

MILITARY ESCORT ATTACKED.

Attempt to Rescue Prisoners.

Mob Armed with Rifles.

DESPERATE ENCOUNTER.

TWO MEN KILLED.

MANY WOUNDED.

Railwaymen's Next Move.

NATIONAL STRIKE THREATENED.

determination to develop cordial relations with the employers and his condemnation of unofficial strikes lowered even further his standing among the rank and file.

In national terms most of the major ports experienced industrial conflict during 1911 and new agreements were reached with employers. In those ports where the NUDL exercised influence such as Hull and Goole on the Humber and Leith in Scotland, agreements were modelled on the Liverpool experience. In London, however, nine separate agreements were necessary to settle affairs and within twelve months a further conflict took place that proved to be disastrous for the London waterside unions.[25]

One further factor requires comment. The Tory Party dominated the Liverpool city council for most of the nineteenth century and the first half of the twentieth century. Politically Liverpool voters were divided on sectarian and ethnic grounds. No radical working class tradition took root in the nineteenth century. Even after the foundation of the Labour Party in 1906 members were deeply divided by sectarian allegiances until after the Second World War. The first Labour councillor was James Sexton, leader of the NUDL, who was elected for the St. Anne's ward in 1905. It was not until the autumn municipal elections following the 1911 strike that the Labour Party successfully established a foothold in the city council when seven candidates were elected. The transport strike encouraged many working class people to vote for Labour candidates when beforehand they had been persuaded to support the traditional parties influenced by sectarian allegiances - or not vote at all. Nevertheless it was not until 1955 that the Labour Party was able to secure a majority of seats on the council.

Notes

1. Major efforts had been made by the unskilled to form unions and to press for higher wages between 1870 and 1875 and from the late 1880s (the period of 'New Unionism'). See K.D. Brown, *The English Labour Movement, 1700-1951* (1982); James Hinton, *Labour and Socialism 1867-1974* (1983); E.H. Hunt, *British Labour History 1815-1914* (1981); D. Kynaston, *King Labour: The British Working Class 1850-1914* (1976); H.A. Clegg, A. Fox and A.F. Thompson, *A History of British Trade Unions since 1889, Vol.1, 1889-1910* (1964).

2. H.M. Pelling, *Popular Politics and Society in Late Victorian Britain* (Second Edition, 1979), p.151.

3. Joe White, '1910-1914 Reconsidered' in J.E. Cronin and J. Schneer (Eds.), *Social Conflict and the Political Order in Modern Britain* (1982), p.80.

4. Speech to members of the Cavendish Club, Bristol, November 1913. Quoted by Lord Askwith in his autobiography *Industrial Problems and Disputes* (1920), p.349.

5. Evidence of Ernest Bevin to the *Court of Inquiry concerning Transport Workers' Wages and Conditions of Employment of Dock Labour* (Shaw Inquiry), 1920, Cmd. 936 and 937. Quoted by G. Brown, *The Industrial Syndicalist* (Spokesman Books, 1974), p.17.

6. Elie Halevy, *A History of the English People in the Nineteenth Century, Vol. VI, The Rule of Democracy, 1905-14* (1934).

7. George Dangerfield, *The Strange Death of Liberal England* (1936), p.viii.

8. Lord Askwith, *op.cit.*, p.350.

9. H.M. Pelling, *Popular Politics*, p.150.

10. Quoted by Pelling, *Ibid*, p.147. Askwith also drew attention to the rise in the cost of living that was not matched by increases in wages.

11. H.A. Clegg, *A History of British Trade Unions since 1889, Vol.II, 1911-1933* (1985), p.73.

The fourteen major strikes analysed by Clegg are as follows:

Date	Strikers	Number of Workers (000s)	Working days lost (000s)
Sept.1910-Aug.1911	Coalminers (Rhondda)	13	2,985
June-Aug.1911	Seamen & Dockers (UK)	120	1,020
July-Aug.1911	Dockers & Carmen (London)	77	500
Aug.1911	Railwaymen (UK)	145	485
Aug.1911	Dockers & Seamen (Liverpool)	48	376
Dec.1911-Jan.1912	Cotton Weavers (NE Lancs)	160	2,954
Feb.-Apr.1912	Coalminers (GB)	1000	30,000
Feb.-Apr.1912	Jute Workers (Dundee)	28	726
May-Aug.1912	Dockers & Carters (London)	100	2,700
Jan.-Mar.1913	Cab Drivers (London)	11	637
Apr.-Jul.1913	Tube & Metal Workers (Midlands)	50	1,400
Aug.1913-Feb.1914	Transport Workers (Dublin)	20	1,900
Jan.-Aug.1914	Construction Workers (London)	20	2,500
Feb.-Apr.1914	Coalminers (Yorkshire)	150	2,654

Source: Clegg, *Ibid*, p.26.

12. G.D.H. Cole and Raymond Postgate, *The Common People* (4th Edition) (1949), p.476.

13. R. Holton, *British Syndicalism 1900-1914. Myths and Realities* (1976).

14. R. Hyman, 'Mass Organisation and Militancy in Britain: Contrasts and Continuities' in Wolfgang J. Mommsen and Hans-Gerhard Husung (Eds.), *The Development of Trade Unionism in Great Britain and Germany, 1880-1914* (1985), p.259.

15. Hyman, *Mass Organisation*, p.262.

16. H.A. Clegg, *op.cit.*, p.25.

17. Margaret Postgate married G.D.H. Cole forming a formidable partnership of left-wing activists, historians, social commentators and detective story writers. The extract is taken from Margaret Cole, *Growing Up into Revolution* (1949), pp.34,35.

18. Philip Gibbs, *The Pageant of the Years* (1946), p125.

19. The Liverpool dock system extended north and south from the Pierhead at the centre of the waterfront. The south end stretched to Toxteth and the north end to Bootle. The south end docks are now closed and the north end docks have been extended to Crosby and Seaforth.

20. Eric Taplin, *The Dockers' Union. A Study of the National Union of Dock Labourers, 1889-1922* (1986), p.95.

21. *Ibid*, p.81.

22. E.L. Taplin, *Liverpool Dockers and Seamen, 1870-1890* (1974), esp. Ch.III.

23. Eric Taplin, *The Dockers' Union*, esp. Ch.4.

24. Eric Taplin, 'False Dawn of New Unionism? Labour Unrest in Liverpool, 1871-73' in John Belchem (Ed.), *Popular Politics, Riot and Labour. Essays in Liverpool History 1790-1940 (1992)*.

25. For events in London see J.C. Lovell, *Stevedores and Dockers. A Study of Trade Unionism in the Port of London 1870-1914* (1969).

The Photographs

A strike of such duration involving so large a proportion of the local labour force was bound to excite public interest. The local daily newspapers devoted several pages of each issue to events of the day which were examined in great detail. While the evening press was largely hostile to the strikers, the two daily papers were sharply divided. The *Daily Courier*, a Tory paper, was usually critical of the workers but the *Daily Post and Mercury*, Liberal in outlook, was more sympathetic. The Labour Correspondent of the *Post* was frequently with the strike leaders and his reports show he was caught up in the enthusiasm for the workers' cause. Major demonstrations took place at the weekends, usually at St. George's Plateau, and during the week there were marches and smaller meetings along the waterfront. During the general strike goods were transported through the city under the escort of police or troops and complaints of food shortages were voiced during August. Even the most indifferent Liverpool citizen must have found it difficult to avoid knowledge of and interest in the dispute. It should also be remembered that the summer of 1911 was exceptionally good. The strike took place during blazing sunshine which encouraged large attendances at marches and demonstrations. An estimated 80,000, for example, turned up for the meeting on Sunday, August 13 that proved to be so disastrous. Some were spectators not directly involved in the strike while many were families out for a day in the sunshine.

Although local interest was considerable, it remains surprising that there is so extensive a photographic record of the dispute. No other major pre-First World War industrial disturbance was so assiduously covered by such a range of photographs. The initiative was taken by the photographic firm of Carbonora which had opened premises in Wilde Street in the city centre, not far from Lime Street railway station, in 1908. During the dispute the firm took 80 photographs which it subsequently issued as a postcard set. They are now, incidentally, a valued collectors' item. The project fitted the policy of the firm of recording important local events and it was, no doubt, caught up in the general excitement that swept across the city. Also the local newspapers used some of its photographs, Carbonora acting as a free-lance agent for the local press.

Many of the photographs are quite outstanding. The scenes of the crowd at St. George's Plateau on 13 August are remarkable for their vividness and sense of occasion. The armoured vehicles used by the police and military, the soldiers - sometimes with fixed bayonets - escorting wagons or arresting rioters, a police charge to dispel hostile crowds, and a gunboat, *HMS Antrim*, moored in the Mersey encapsulate the sense of crisis pervading the city. The lines of empty trams and the frustrated passengers at railway stations exemplify the impact of the general strike upon the normal life of the city. The extremes of wealth and poverty of early twentieth century Liverpool are captured almost by accident: the ragged, barefoot children of dockland contrasting sharply with the well-dressed would-be passengers at Lime Street railway station.

This is, therefore, a remarkable collection. Nevertheless the photographic record of the dispute is incomplete and there are some omissions that render the set less valuable than it might have been. The firm began to take photographs when the railwaymen's agitation developed in August. The waterfront dispute from mid-June to early August is not recorded. We can scarcely appreciate from the firm's photographs that seafarers and waterfront workers were at the heart of the conflict. There are no photographs of seafarers in the collection. Most of the photographs of the strikers in procession are of railwaymen and tramwaymen. The latter group in particular receives undue emphasis.

More surprising, however, there is no photograph of the debacle at St. George's Plateau on August 13. It seems inconceivable that the photographer(s) having taken at least six pictures of the vast crowds assembled should have left before the police intervened. The sight of the police baton-charging the crowd, the general disorder and the Plateau littered with bricks, bottles and the injured when the police had completed their task would be a press photographer's dream. That night and for the following few days street fighting and looting took place yet there is only one photograph of the police being stoned and chasing their attackers. The evidence points to censorship. Some of the photographs must have been deemed too alarming by the civil or military authorities and were probably suppressed.

Not all the photographs in the collection are of equal interest. Those showing convoys of wagons with police and military escort are repetitive. They illustrate the tense situation but suggest that law and order prevailed. Only two plates show the strikers seeking to halt the movement of goods. The many incidents of this kind were ignored or missed by the photographer(s) or were censored in the interests of public order.

There are said to be 80 photographs in the complete set although only 73 of the original postcards from which the photographs have been processed are held in the Liverpool Central Libraries (Record Office). Additional photographs from the local press, not found within the Carbonora collection have been included where they bring to light additional material of interest. The *Sphere*, a London magazine, in its issues of August 1911 published a number of photographs and drawings of the Liverpool dispute. Some of these have also been included.

The photographs have been arranged in three sections: the strikers, the forces of law and order and miscellaneous. A fourth section of documents has been included. Each photograph and document has an explanatory caption.

The Carbonora photographic firm has a continuous history from 1870 although it now operates under the name of John Mills Photography Ltd. It was founded by Thomas Mills in Bangor, North Wales, and has remained a family firm. Thomas Mills' four sons moved the business to Liverpool in 1908, opening premises in Wilde Street. Gwilym Mills remained in charge of the Wilde Street business while two of his brothers opened separate photographic firms, one in Walton, a suburb of Liverpool (trading under the name of Dorondo), and one in London Road, near the city centre. The remaining brother emigrated to America. Thus the initiative to record the 1911 dispute was taken by Gwilym Mills and it is fitting that he is featured in the photograph on page 82.

After the First World War Gwilym Mills moved the firm from Wilde Street to Lime Street, in the city centre. In 1941, the premises were bombed during the Liverpool blitz and all the records and photographic plates stored there were destroyed. The firm overcame this disaster by concentrating its activities in Walton and by opening new premises in Windermere in the Lake District. The Windermere outlet was sold shortly after the war.

Gwilym Mills remained in charge of the firm until his retirement in 1950. He was succeeded as managing director by his son, John Mills, who changed the name of the firm to John Mills Photography Ltd. and, in 1960, acquired premises in Hope Street.

On the accession of John Mills the policy of the firm changed. From its early days in Liverpool Gwilym Mills had concentrated on the profitable activity of recording social events on Merseyside, processing them as postcards and distributing them to local newsagents, etc. Carbonora was also the official photographer for the Liverpool police force. The relationship with the Merseyside police has been retained but the firm now concentrates on industrial photography. The Mills group of companies is still very involved with the life of Liverpool and has produced a series of video productions on the regeneration of the city. The Mills Video Company is managed by Andrew Mills, the fourth generation of the family to practice photography.

Today we take for granted the instantaneous transmission of news on a world-wide basis. In an age before radio and television and when newspaper photography was restricted and the cinema in its infancy, a detailed visual record of a major industrial disturbance was unknown. That is what makes the Carbonora postcard set unique and invaluable.

Abbreviations used in the commentary to the photographs and documents.

ASE *Amalgamated Society of Engineers*

Carbonora *Carbonora postcard collection*

Carters' Union *Mersey Quay and Railway Carters' Union*

HH *Harold Hikins' documentary collection*

LDPM Liverpool Daily Post and Mercury

LRO *Liverpool Record Office*

LWP Liverpool Weekly Post

NAUL *National Amalgamated Union of Labour*

NMGM *National Museums and Galleries on Merseyside*

NUDL *National Union of Dock Labourers in Great Britain and Ireland*

NSFU *National Sailors' and Firemen's Union*

Sphere The Sphere *magazine*

Stewards' Union *National Union of Ships' Stewards, Cooks, Butchers and Bakers*

TGWU *Transport and General Workers' Union*

The Strikers

The strike began June 14, 1911 when the seamen struck work. Since 1910 Joseph Havelock Wilson, the president of the National Seamen's and Firemen's Union (NSFU), had been seeking without success to negotiate with the shipping employers on a national basis to secure a National Conciliation Board to discuss a variety of issues including a national minimum wage and improved manning scales. This would have involved recognition of the union and the employers flatly rejected Wilson's overtures. The union prepared for a national strike but the men in a number of ports walked out in June 1911 and Wilson hastily declared the strike official. The seamen (deckhands) and firemen (stokehold men) were quickly followed by stewards and catering staff. This was unprecedented as the stewards looked upon themselves as superior to the seamen. Joe Cotter, who had been a steward on Cunard ships, had formed the National Union of Ships' Stewards, Cooks, Butchers and Bakers in 1909 and the men were now able to express their grievances through union organisation especially the use of cheap foreign labour.

Opposite The photograph shows a mass meeting of seafarers at Birkenhead Park Gates. D. J. Kenny, local secretary of the NSFU, is introducing Tom Mann. (LDPM)

Left A. Despres of the Stewards' Union addressing a meeting of seamen at the Alexandra Dock at the north end of the Liverpool dock system. (LDPM)

Below *Some of the big shipping companies like Cunard and the White Star Line granted concessions but the smaller firms, mainly concerned with cargo traffic, were reluctant to concede pay rises and there was considerable confusion. A groundswell of support for the seafarers developed among other waterfront workers and the dockers, carters and coalheavers walked out on sympathetic strike following a demonstration at St. George's Plateau on Sunday 25 June attended by some 3-4,000 transport workers.*

Many dock workers were members of the National Union of Dock Labourers (NUDL) which had been formed in 1889. It had been recognised by most firms at the south end of the docks and by smaller firms at the north end but the giant firms with reserved berths at the north end had successfully resisted the union presence. Any man found belonging to the union was instantly dismissed. Yet when the seafarers struck work it was the non-union dockers who were the most militant in their sympathetic support. In any case they formulated demands of their own within days and flocked to join the union in defiance of their employers.

The carters were organised in the Mersey Quay and Railway Carters' Union which had been formed in 1889. They enjoyed amicable relationships with their employers and their sympathetic strike action came as a surprise.

Coalheavers were the men who loaded the steamships with coal, a back-breaking and dangerous job. They were organised in two unions, one representing the north end men the other the south end workers. Some 2,000 coalheavers turned out in support of the seafarers and they were followed by unorganised waterfront workers such as cold storage workers and boiler scalers.

The photograph shows a meeting of dock workers at the Canada Dock gates at the north end. (LDPM)

Left *Tom Mann was a key figure in the dispute. He was a skilled engineer but during the 1880s became an advocate of militant trade unionism especially among the unorganised unskilled workers. He was a major figure in the famous London dock strike of 1889 and became president of the London Dockers' Union. He was a committed socialist and, by 1911, a syndicalist urging workers' control of industry through direct action. He emphasised the importance of industrial solidarity during the Liverpool strike which proved to be a major factor in the ultimate victory of the workers. He enjoyed an international reputation as a superb orator, fearless in his advocacy of improving the conditions of work and standard of living of working people through trade union organisation. He arrived in Liverpool the day before the strike began, was elected chairman of the strike committee (see pages 28 and 55) and was the major tactician throughout the conflict.*

D. J. Kenny, local secretary of the NSFU, was a Birkenhead councillor for several years and a member of the local Marine Board. Tragically the strain of the conflict led to his admission to the Royal Infirmary where he died on 14 August 1911.

W. Frazer was a local official of the Amalgamated Society of Engineers (ASE).

In the photograph Kenny is on the left, Frazer in the middle and Mann is on the right. (LDPM)

Above The first phase of the strike was confined to the waterfront and the strike committee was composed of representatives of the unions of waterside workers. As the strike escalated so the committee expanded to include representatives of all the unions involved (see page 55). This photograph shows the initial committee.

Back Row (standing from left to right): J. Connor (NSFU), G. Ruffler (NSFU), J. Stephenson (president, Stewards' Union and member of the Liverpool Trades Council).

Second Row (from left to right): J. Hesson (NSFU), J. Cotter (Secretary, Stewards' Union), D. J. Kenny (Liverpool secretary, NSFU), T. Dixon (NSFU), Jack Wood (NUDL).

Front Row (from left to right): Frank Pierce (assistant secretary, Stewards' Union), Thomas Ditchfield (secretary, Carters' Union), Tom Mann (chairman), James Sexton (general secretary, NUDL), A. Despres (Stewards' Union). (LDPM)

Left to page 33 By 4 August the waterfront dispute appeared to have been resolved. But by then the railwaymen were increasingly restive demanding a reduction in hours and increased wages. This was a national movement but in the highly-charged atmosphere in Liverpool some 4,000 railway workers came out on strike on 7 August. The strike committee supported them and in a declaration of solidarity decided to bring out all transport workers in sympathy. The shipping employers reacted angrily by threatening to suspend all cargo operations and thus locking out the men. The ill-fated demonstration of 13 August - Bloody Sunday - precipitated a general transport strike that brought the city to a virtual standstill.

These eight photographs record the vast crowd assembling at St. George's Plateau. Blue collar workers are identified by their caps. Stewards and white collar workers wore either straw boaters or bowler hats. The banners of the unions were much in evidence. *(Carbonora, except top left Sphere)*

Below Cricket continued even in the midst of the strike! (NMGM - Carbonora)

The events of Bloody Sunday soured relationships between the working people and the civil authorities made more acute by 2,000 troops being rushed to the city. The highly-charged atmosphere encouraged rioting and looting and many arrests were made.

The two photographs show a fire in Standish Street. (Carbonora)

Below *The artist of this drawing, F. Matania, witnessed this scene from his hotel bedroom in Christian Street, Liverpool. The strikers are arming themselves with bricks by demolishing a wall. The horse on the ground was shot dead by a soldier after its leg had been broken by a missile. Although the strikes were among predominantly male occupations this drawing shows that women played an important role in supporting their men. (Sphere)*

Below & opposite *These three photographs show Tom Mann addressing a meeting of dockers. In the bottom photograph Frank Kilkelly, secretary of the Bootle branch (No. 3) of the NUDL is on Mann's right and George Milligan, secretary of the North End branch (No. 12) is next to him.*

Kilkelly was a long serving officer of the NUDL. Originally from Dublin he joined the union on its foundation in 1889 becoming the first

DRAWN IN LIVERPOOL BY F. MATANIA

THE GREAT STRIKES IN LIVERPOOL— RIOTERS ARMING THEMSELVES WITH AMMUNITION

A scene in Christian Street actually witnessed by our artist. The name of the street has an irony of its own. It will be observed that the rioters are breaking down a wall for weapons of warfare against the police and that a woman is assisting by carrying bricks in her apron. The horse was shot by a soldier after its leg had been broken by

secretary of the Bootle branch, a position he held until his death in 1916. He was deeply religious with a strong commitment to Irish Home Rule. Although a poor public speaker he was a popular and well-respected branch secretary.

George Milligan rose from obscurity to a position of importance in the NUDL as a result of the strike. He was a dock porter, a specialist checker, working for the White Star Line. He formed a semi-clandestine branch of the union at the north end in 1908 and was looked upon as a hero by the non-union dockers who worked for the great liner companies. He was a devout catholic (of some importance as the majority of catholic dockers worked at the north end) and was admired for his courage and integrity. He was appointed deputy general secretary of the NUDL in 1919. When the NUDL was absorbed in the TGWU in 1922 he became Mersey Area Secretary until his death in 1925. (Carbonora)

A DANGER-SPOT IN LIVERPOOL : When Visible Force Meets the Worker on Strike.

Left As Tom Mann was addressing the crowd so a convoy passed by under police and military escort. The troops have fixed bayonets. The civilian at the head of the infantry is a magistrate with the power to read the Riot Act should it become necessary. (Sphere)
Below A crowd outside the Buckingham Hotel where windows had been smashed after a riot the previous evening. (LDPM)
Opposite Broken windows of the Shakespeare public house in Christian Street. (Carbonora)

Top Police being stoned as they baton-charge a crowd. (Carbonora)

Bottom left Police besieged in a tenement building being stoned by a crowd. (LDPM)

Bottom right The siege is raised as police manage to rescue their colleagues. (LDPM)

Top An arrested striker being escorted by police. (Sphere)

Bottom left The police are less charitable to this striker who is being frog-marched away. (Sphere)

Bottom right A picket being arrested. The photographer entitled the picture 'A tough customer'. (Carbonora)

Top left *An arrest in Byrom Street. Notice the military escort with fixed bayonets. (LDPM)*

Above *A prisoner being escorted to the Bridewell. Six mounted police had to assist to prevent a rescue. (LDPM)*

Opposite *Three prisoners being escorted by police to the Bridewell. (Carbonora)*

Bottom left *Mounted police clearing the way in Tunnel Road, Edgehill. (Carbonora)*

Opposite top *Police and Scots Greys clear the streets.* (Sphere) **Opposite bottom** *The Lusitania moored in the Mersey, held up by the dispute.* (Sphere)

Above *When the strike committee declared a general transport strike the shipowners locked out the men on 14 August. But this photograph shows that some 100 men turned up to work on the Lusitania. They were turned away.* (LDPM)

Left *There were two deaths during the strike. Troops escorting prison vans to Walton Gaol followed an unaccustomed route through the dock area. They were attacked by 'a mob' and in clearing the streets two men were killed. This photograph shows the house of John Sutcliffe, a protestant carter, in Hopwood Street, off Vauxhall Road. His sister alleged that he was putting up the shutters of his house when he was killed by a stray bullet. X marks the spot where he fell. The ragged clothing of the working class children is in sharp contrast to the dress of the passengers stranded at Lime Street station (see page 85). (Carbonora)*

Above *Carters' boys at the London and North Western Railway Company's station at Edgehill. (Carbonora)*

Opposite top *This photograph shows the junction of Hopwood Street and Vauxhall Road. X marks the spot where Michael Prendegast, a catholic dock worker, was shot dead by the troops in the incident described above. The houses at the Vauxhall Road end of Hopwood Street have now been demolished and that part of the street renamed Gem Street but the pub on the corner is still there, now The Jamaica. (Carbonora)*

Right *The funeral cortege of Michael Prendegast on its way to the Ford catholic cemetery. The Post reporter commented that 'the procession through the streets was a sad one, the hearse and carriages being followed by hundreds of sympathisers and friends, whilst immense crowds of poor people thronged the streets to watch the cortege pass. Among those in the procession were 250 members of the Netherfield Road Protestant Reformers' Crusade who also sent wreaths.' At John Sutcliffe's funeral 150 members of the Catholic Defence League were in the procession. Sectarian strife, for so long an ugly feature of Liverpool's social and political life, was subsumed by those involved in the conflict in the interests of solidarity. Minor riots between catholics and protestants that occurred after Bloody Sunday were confined to the most bigoted and probably were initiated by those who were not involved in the strike. (LWP)*

Top *'Tired strikers' take a rest on the steps of St. George's Hall. (Carbonora)*

Bottom *A meeting of strikers at Edgehill. (Carbonora)*

Opposite top *Strikers outside Canada Dock station at the north end of the dock system. (Carbonora)*

Below Strikers at the London and North Western Railway company's works at Wavertree. The men climbing over the wall into the works are hoping to persuade those still at work to join them. (Carbonora)

Right Strikers preventing the progress of wagons in Regent Road near Canada Dock station. (*Carbonora*)

Opposite top On 17 August a large proportion of the corporation tramwaymen struck work quickly followed by men employed at the corporation electric power station in Lister Drive and the scavengers (street cleaners and dustmen). This photograph shows empty trams in Lime Street. (*Carbonora*)

Opposite bottom Not all tramwaymen turned out. This photograph shows a tram being stopped in Derby Road, Liverpool by strikers. (*Sphere*)

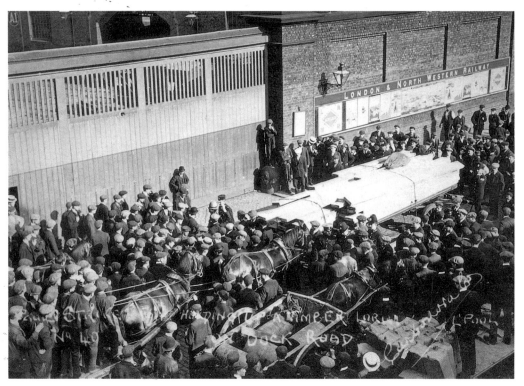

LPOOL STRIKE 68.
DESERTED CARS IN *Lime St.* Cartonora Lpool

*These four photographs show the progress of a march by tramwaymen and dockers to the city centre. **Top left** shows the procession passing by Cabbage Hall in Lower Breck Road. **Bottom left** is taken in Mount Pleasant. The tramwaymen, in uniform, are to the right of the picture, the dockers in the centre and left. **Top right** shows the procession in Lord Street. The placard refers to management reports that only 250 men had turned out while the men claimed there were 1,000. **Bottom right** the procession has reached Paradise Street in the city centre. (Carbonora)*

TRAMWAY STRIKERS.

Opposite *Tramwaymen resting after their demonstration. (Carbonora)*
Above *The final strike committee. As the strike spread so the committee was enlarged to represent all trade unions involved. Compare this photograph with the initial committee (page 28).*

Back Row *(standing from left to right): J. Bromley (affiliation unknown); T. Williamson (NAUL); W. Edwards (Operative Bakers' Union); W.H.B. Quilliam (vice-president, Carters' Union); A.W. Short (Stewards' Union); James Connolly (affiliation unknown, possibly J. Connor (NSFU)); A.J. Williams (ASRS); R.H. Allen (Dock Board Coopers' Union).*

Second Row *(standing from left to right): H. McDonagh (affiliation unknown); W.H. Jones (Carters' Union); Ed. Lamb (ASE); J. Cotter*

(secretary, Stewards' Union); J. Hanratty (Coalheavers' Union); George Milligan (NUDL); W. Murray (NUDL); M. McGrath (NUDL); Jack Wood (NUDL); J. Phipps (affiliation unknown).

Third Row *(sitting from left to right): Frank Kilkelly (NUDL); T. Chambers (NSFU); J. Stephenson (president, Stewards' Union and member of the Liverpool Trades Council); Tom Mann (chairman); James Sexton (general secretary, NUDL); T. Ditchfield (secretary, Carters' Union); P. Kean (South End Coalheavers' Union); P. Casey (North End Coalheavers' Union).*

Fourth Row *(sitting from left to right): J. Hessom (NSFU); R.F. Bell (NSFU); J.W. Clarke (treasurer, Warehousemen's Union); J. Dickson (NSFU); J.W. Gardner (Navvies & General Labourers' Union). (ASE)*

The Forces Of Law And Order

Top *Up until Bloody Sunday there had been little violence considering the numbers on strike. Nevertheless as tension grew so the civil authorities secured extra police from Leeds and Birmingham and a contingent of soldiers of the 2nd Warwickshire Regiment was moved to Seaforth Barracks. The photograph shows Birmingham police arriving in the city. (Carbonora)*

Bottom *A contingent of police marching through Liverpool. (Carbonora)*

Two photographs of police outside the Dale Street Bridewell. (Carbonora)

L'POOL ST.
THE STIPENDARY & COL EAST
19

CARSON L'POOL. L'POOL STRIKE No 31. L'POOL STIPENDARY AND ASS CONSTABL

Opposite *Stuart Deacon, Colonel East and Francis Coldwell, Assistant Chief Constable. (Carbonora)*

Following the disaster of Bloody Sunday and the subsequent rioting and looting two thousand extra troops were rushed to the city. These next five photographs show: (a) troops of the 18th Hussars camped at Edge Lane estate (page 61); (b) the Hussars on parade outside the corporation tramway office in Hatton Garden in the city centre (page 62); (c) men of the Scots Greys (pages 63, 64). (Carbonora)

STRIKE 95 SCOTCH GREYS AWAITING ORDERS   Carbonora L'Pool

Below A docker puts his case to the soldiers.

Opposite On 19 August HMS Antrim appeared in the Mersey and was moored there for a few days before it sailed away as quietly as it had arrived. (Carbonora)

STRIKE 1911

No: 5 Y.

H.M.S. "ANTRIM" IN READINESS

Carbonora Lpool.

Top When a general transport strike was declared after Bloody Sunday the city came to a near standstill. The strike committee issued permits for the movement of goods. Tom Mann declared that they would be confined to milk, 'the child's staple diet', and bread, 'the staff of life'. Other goods could, therefore, only be transported under heavy police escort. This photograph shows a convoy under mounted police escort in Sefton Street at the south end of the docks. The overhead railway (the dockers' umbrella) which ran the length of the docks is in the background. The overhead railway was finally closed in 1958. (Carbonora)

Bottom A convoy with police and military escort in Dock Road. (Carbonora)

Opposite A convoy with military and police escort passing the Mersey Forge Engine Works in Sefton Street. Note that the soldiers have fixed bayonets. (Carbonora)

A convoy with mounted police escort in Church Street in the city centre. (Carbonora)

Top A convoy with police escort in Victoria Street in the city centre. (Carbonora)
Bottom Police escorting a wagon in Lime Street. (Carbonora)

Top Right *Convoy with police escort crossing Lime Street from St. John's Lane. St. George's Hall is on the right of the picture. (Carbonora)*

Bottom right *A contingent of the 18th Hussars escorting a convoy as it turns into London Road from Lime Street. (Carbonora)*

Below *Mounted police near St. George's Hall patrolling the streets. (Sphere)*

Opposite *Troops and police in Whitechapel. (Carbonora)*

DETACHMENT IN WHITECHAPEL.

Above *A wagon of flour being moved under permit from the strike committee.* (Sphere)

Bottom left *A medicine cart under permit from the strike committee.* (Sphere)

Bottom right *Fears of food shortages arose as the conflict persisted. Williamson Square in the city centre contained cold storage facilities and became the distribution point for the transport of perishable goods under military and police escort. This photograph shows a convoy preparing to move off.* (LWP)

Opposite *Troops escorting police in armoured vehicles.* (Carbonora)

Opposite *Scots Greys in Edge Lane. (Carbonora)*

Left *A convoy under police and military escort. (NMGM - probably Carbonora)*

Opposite *A convoy being prepared under escort by the Scots Greys. (NMGM - Carbonora)*
Left *Convoy under escort passing Edgehill Station. (Carbonora)*

Scots Greys escorting police vans along County Road, Walton. (Carbonora)

LPOOL STRIKE. 59
ARMOURED IN LPOOL

Top *Armoured police van in Rice Lane, Walton. (Carbonora)*

Bottom *A police van carrying police and troops in Lister Drive where the electric power station was sited. (Carbonora)*

Left *Armoured police vans.*
(Carbonora)

CARBONORA Co:
L'POOL.

L'POOL STRIKE 62.

ON ENTRY AT EXCHANGE

Opposite *'Bringing in stores by armoured motor' to the Dale Street police headquarters. Gwilym Mills, owner of Carbonora, is the civilian in the centre of the photograph. (Carbonora)*

Above *A sentry on duty outside Exchange Station in Tithebarn Street in the city centre. (Carbonora)*

When the strike drew to its close the Leeds and Birmingham police were withdrawn. These photographs show the Birmingham police before their departure and marching into Lime Street station on their way home. (Carbonora)

Stranded travellers at Lime Street station during the railwaymen's strike. (Carbonora)

Top *A horse collapses in Tunnel Road at the junction with Leeds Street. (Carbonora)*

Bottom *The government sought to avoid direct involvement in the strike though it authorised the movement of troops and extra police into the city at the request of the civil authorities. By mid-August, however, there were fears of food shortages and on 18 August the Home Secretary appointed a Conciliation Commission to make recommendations 'to restore better relations between the various classes' and 'in consultation with the Lord Mayor report on the food supply and general position in the city'. The members of the commission were, from left to right, T.P. O'Connor, Nationalist MP for the Scotland Division of Liverpool, D.J. Shackleton, Labour Advisor to the Home Office, and Colonel Kyffin Taylor, Conservative MP for the Kirkdale Division of Liverpool. The strike ended a week after their appointment and their deliberations had no effect on the resolution of the dispute. (Carbonora)*

Documents

Document 1 Joseph Havelock Wilson was the leader of the Seamen's Union. This letter to Tom Mann, the chairman of the strike committee in Liverpool, was written at the end of the first week of the seamen's strike. It illustrates the *national* nature of the seamen's struggle to secure higher wages and improved conditions of work. Wilson was clearly apprehensive that the strike would fail if success was not achieved rapidly. He also shows some contempt for the rank and file. The comments in the margin and the underlinings were made by Tom Mann. (HH)

20th June 1911

Dear Tom Mann,

I was so pleased to have your letter of 19th. I am sorry to say that the effects of the fight is being felt on my poor body, but I will never surrender. Now will you please keep before you the fact that we are in an international fight, and that it is not possible to maintain the same position im everyone of the ports. There are some places where we are weak and in other places some of our leaders are not blessed with too much intelligence. I want you to understand that my policy as well as yours is fight, fight, fight, but circumstances may arise in some places where we will have to alter our policy a little bit. If I could depend on every centre and the men, I can assure you that nothing would satisfy me but the absolute break up entirely of the Shipping Federation, and nothing less than a minimum wage of £6 per month - I know the material with which we have to work. They are shifty and uncertain and very bold and courageous at the wrong time and pig headed in doing what you want. For instance on Friday things looked shaky in London The Anglo American Oil Co. had a boat at Purfleet. The Captain rung up and offered me £5 for sailors and £5.10 for firemen. I agreed to accept this which mean (sic) an advance of 10/- seeing that victories had not come in our road in London up till late last Friday night. The men called on me and agreed to accept this, but when they got down to the ship, one or two sore heads persuaded them to demand the wages according to the bill, viz., £5'10. sailors and £6 firemen. The Company wouldn't pay. The result is that to-day the 20th, the vessel had practically lost 5 days. I got another crew to go down to her last night, the other fellows laid wait for them and stopped them from signing, so she is still lying there. If we could only get the men to trust implicitly in their leaders and obey, all would be well There is a time when you can put the steam on, and there is a time when you ought to ease up.

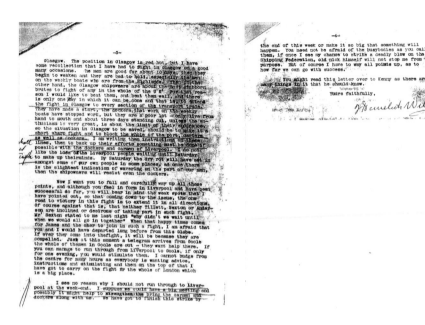

Now, my dear Tom, looking at the reports from every quarter this morning, the position is exceedingly strong, but I am afraid that unless we take drastic steps, the next 24 hours will show a great weakness. Take for instance the Bristol Channel. Although the men hitherto have been strong and loyal, up to the present time they have not recorded six victories, and the men who handed in their books are now clamouring to have them returned. I know Cardiff down to the ground and this shows that the rot has already begun to set in, in Cardiff. Now I do not mean that all the men will desert, but there will be sufficient to leave us, to allow the Cardiff shipowners to get their vessels away without being affected and then it is only a question of time when the other men in the Bristol Channel ports will follow suit.

The Humber ports at this moment are in a very strong position and likely to gain strength for the next 48 hours, as Butchers men have sent an ultimatum to the owners, that unless they get a settlement in the wages by 10 o'clock to-day, Tuesday, they cease work. They are a very pig headed, strong minded type of men. There is nothing flabby about them, and when they fight, they fight, so that Hull will feel the effects for the next 48 hours, and there may be a chance of the Dockers or some of them catching the fever, and further developments may be expected in the Humber.

Goole at this moment is solid, the sailors and firemen are all Yorkshiremen and they are out for blood and they have left their ships manfully. The coal trimmers have joined in with them. I am going to advise the extension of the fight in Goole, only I am treading on dangerous ground These men belong to Sexton and he is already resenting what we have done in bringing his men out.

N.E. Coast. The position along the N'E' Coast ports is very strong. Weekly boat men everywhere have got 35/- a week. The few boats that refused have been successfully hung up. The feeling amongst the men is full of enthusiasm, and I have not much fear of the N'E' Coast ports for the next 5 days.

Leith. I am a bit afraid of the position' So far the men have responded well on the weekly boats and a considerable number are detained, and others may be detained within the next 24 hours, but unfortunately we have not anybody of a forcible character leading the fight in Leith. So far the man in charge there has done well. Our policy should be if I could get someone to go, to bring the dockers along with us they do not belong to any organization, but my difficulty is to get men to send on such expeditions. Therefore although Leith stands good at this moment, I am somewhat shaky as to its continuance.

Glasgow. The position in Glasgow is red hot, but I have some recollection that I have had to fight in Glasgow on a good many occasions. The men are good for about 10 days, then they begin to weaken and they are bad to hold, especially the men on the weekly boats who are from the Highlands. Then on the other hand, the Glasgow shipowners are about the most stubborn brutes to fight of any in the whole of the U'K' For that reason I would like to beat them, and beat them well, and there is only one way in which it can be done and that is, to extend the fight in Glasgow to every section of the transport trade. They have made a start, the dockers that work on the weekly boats have stopped work, but they are a poor lot - only live from hand to mouth and about three days standing out, unless the enthusiasm is very great, is about the limit of their endurance, so the situation in Glasgow to be saved, should be to make it a short sharp fight and to block the whole of the port, carters as well as dockers. I am writing them instructions on these lines, then to back up their efforts something must be done if possible with the dockers and carmen of Liverpool. I do not like the idea of the Liverpool people waiting until Saturday to make up their minds. By Saturday the dry rot will have set in amongst some of our own people in some places, ad (sic) once there is the slightest indication of wavering on the part of our men, then the shipowners will resist even the dockers.

Now I want you to full and carefully way (sic) up all these points, and although you feel in form in Liverpool and have been successful so far, you will bear in mind the weak spots that I have pointed out, so that coming down to the issue, the one road to victory in this fight is to extend it in all directions. Of course against that is, that neither Tillett, Sexton or Anderson are inclined or desirous of taking part in such fight. Mr' Sexton stated to me last night "why didn't we wait until when we would all go in together" When that happy times (sic)

comes for James and the oher (sic) to join in such a fight, I am afraid that you and I would have departed long before from this Globe. If ever they come into the fight, it will be because they are compelled. Just at this moment a telegram arrives from Goole the whole of the men in Goole are out - they want help there. If you can manage to run through from Liverpool to Goole, if only for one evening, you would stimulate them. I cannot budge from the centre for many hours as everybody is wanting advice, instructions and stimulating and then on the top of that I have got to carry on the fight for the whole of London which is a big place.

I see no reason why I should not run through to Liverpool at the week-end. I suppose we could have a big meeting and possibly it might help to bring the carmen and dockers along with us. We have got to finish this strike by the end of this week or make it so big that something will happen. You need not be afraid of the busybodies as you call them, if once I see my chance to strike a deadly blow on the Shipping Federation, old nick himself will not stop me from the purpose. But of course I have to way (sic) all points up, as to how far we can go with success.

You might read this letter over to Kenny as there are many things in it that he should know.

Yours faithfully,

(sgd.) J Havelock Wilson

Document 2 When the general strike was declared in August and goods could only be moved without trouble if the strike committee issued permits, many firms wrote to Mann seeking permits for safe passage. This letter from the Chief Postmaster of Liverpool sought to secure movement of mail carts. His request was granted. As the photographs illustrate firms who were refused permits could move goods only under heavy police and military escort. (HH)

Liverpool, 14th August 1911.

Sir,
You are reported in this morning's Liverpool papers to have said yesterday that a general strike of transport workers would commence to-morrow morning if a satisfactory settlement of the dispute were not arrived at this morning. I have just learned that the Docks have been closed and all work in them suspended. It is not definitely stated whether the Mail Cart Drivers are included in the expression "transport workers", and I shall be obliged therefore if you will be good enough to inform me whether the free passage of the Mail Carts conveying mails will be objected to or the Drivers interfered with.
I may add that in making this application I am directed particularly to explain, for the information of your Committee, that it is not within the province of the Postmaster General to interfere and that he has no desire to interfere in any way in the conduct of the Strike whether on behalf of the employer or employed. The only object in view in this communication to you is to secure if possible the regular continuance of Mail Services,

which cannot be interrupted without the gravest inconvenience to the residents of the whole of the city and suburbs.
The bearer of this letter will give any information you may desire as to the conditions of employment of the Mail Cart Drivers, and I shall be obliged if you will be good enough to send your reply by him.

I am,
Your obedient Servant,
(sgd.) F. Salisbury
Liverpool, 14th August 1911.

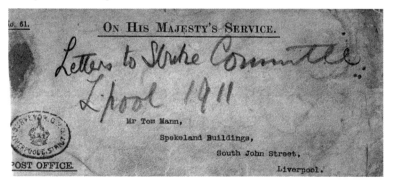

Sir,
I beg to thank you for your letter intimating that the Mail cart services will not be interfered with.

I am, Sir,
Your obedient Servant,
(sgd.) F. Salisbury
Mr T. Mann.

Document 3 These two notes from the Toxteth Cooperative Society illustrate the support for the strike by working people not directly involved. (HH)

19th August 1911

Gentlemen,

I enclose you a copy of a resolution passed by our Committee on Wednesday evening last, which may be of interest to you.
A copy of this resolution was posted to the Editors of our local papers, but up to the present does not appear to have been published.
We thank you for the "Permits" which you have supplied us with, and they have been a great help to us.

Yours faithfully,
(sgd.) Joseph Kitchen
Gen: Manager & Secty.

Encl:

Co-operative and the Liverpool Strike.

At a meeting of the Committee of the Toxteth Co-operative Society it was resolved that "On behalf of the Members we desire to record our sympathy with the men on strike in their effort to improve their conditions of labour, and trust that an early amicable settlement will ensue".

Document 4 This is a letter from Tom Mann to his wife, Elsie. It illustrates his confidence, determination and good humour. Kenney, referred to in the letter, was the local seamen's leader (see Plate 4). (HH)

Transcript of Document 4: letter from Tom Mann to his wife.

29 Bradfield St
Edge Lane
L'pool

Friday 7.20 a.m.
18 Aug 1911

My dear Elsie
I am still alright no accident & in perfect health. You will know that matters have developed here, culminating yesterday with the stoppage of the trams & serious reduction of eletric light, to day the overhead Railway will stop and the Dock Gates are closed (by us) all along the line. Liverpool is tied up. As fast as they brought military we applied the Strike & yesterday they brought the battleship "Antrim" & two more will or have by now arrived, and still "Solidarity" beats them all. You will I think remember I told you about my talking with Hardie in H. of Com. when Lansbury came along, & when I briefly expounded Industrialism he expressed his regret & said I "had gone back 40 years." Well he Lansbury wired us from Parmt about the Police charges so he came down for a few hours yesterday & expressed his utter astonishment at what we have been able to do & how impossible he thought it to be when I spoke to him in Parmt. Well the Railways will stop to day unless anything happened in London late last night to avoid it. The four Railwaymens Societies jointly sent the instruction to their branches by wire, it cost over £1000 to do it - so many branches; this in itself is a great achievement, so much greater than seemed possible even three weeks ago that the men who have agreed upon Common action seem astonished at themselves. By many tradesmen here I am looked upon as a Dictator because my signature opens a clear way for them to get provisions & they dont turn to the Authorities & ask for Convoy which they cd (sic) get, the Strike Committee permit is of greater value. It is not merely amusing but a powerful object lesson to see a Military convoy escorting three wagons some 300 men often to guard it, then another three come along with a Strike Committee Authorisation & not a person with them but the Carters. Lord Mayor, Head Constable, Police, special Constables, Military & gun boats all sink into insignificance by the side of working class solidarity, and even a fool can see it in operation at this hour in this City.

That in the Dy Mail which I sent yesterday was really an interview not an article, but it gets there pretty well, & their article is not too bad, the admissions are most sygnificant (sic).

Of course I have to walk to & from town, & in addition yesterday I went to the funeral of one of our Committeemen, David Kenney the Sailors Sec, the man who first wrote me from Liverpool about my being requested to act down here, he underwent an operation & died & the funeral march was three miles long each way. He was a Municipal Councillor & a great man with the Catholics, & ceremonies were on a big scale. I can't get to Eccles for Sunday a taxi wd cost fully £3 & I suppose much more by waiting time.

I suppose this deadlock will last another couple of days & then negotiations will commence. I dont think we need worry. Hope you had a nice day a Thorpes Bay. I wish you could have had a week.

Best love to all
Dada

Troops with fixed bayonets protect a convoy through the city. (NMGM)

Documents 5-6 During the strike the city authorities enrolled volunteers as special constables. When the electric power station workers turned out blacklegs were recruited to maintain electricity supplies. When the dispute ended certificates were issued to the volunteers for services rendered to the community. (LRO)

I hereby Certify that Ernest D. Edwards served as a Special Constable during a period of tumult and riot arising out of the Strikes and labour disputes in August, 1911.
On behalf of the Justices of the Peace of the City, I tender to him their thanks for his services to the community.

Lord Mayor and Chief Magistrate of the City.

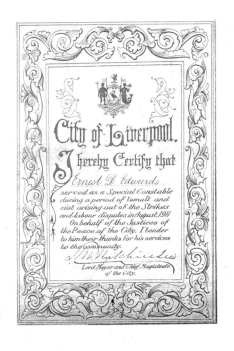

I hereby Certify that E.D. Edwards rendered assistance as a Voluntary Worker at Lister Drive Electric Power Station during the Strike in August, 1911.
On behalf of the Tramways and Electric Power and Lighting Committee, I tender to him the thanks of the Committee for the valuable services rendered by him to the Committee and to the community at large.

Lord Mayor